The Fishery Laws...

Frederick Pollock

The Great International Fisheries Exhibition

(230)

THE

FISHERY LAWS

BY

FREDERICK POLLOCK

BARRISTER-AT-LAW, M.A., HON. LL.D. EDIN.
CORPUS CHRISTI PROFESSOR OF JURISPRUDENCE IN THE UNIVERSITY OF OXFORD
LATE FELLOW OF TRINITY COLLEGE, CAMBRIDGE

LONDON
WILLIAM CLOWES AND SONS, LIMITED
INTERNATIONAL FISHERIES EXHIBITION
AND 13 CHARING CROSS, S.W.
1883

LONDON:
PRINTED BY WILLIAM CLOWES AND SONS, Limited,
STAMFORD STREET AND CHARING CROSS.

TABLE OF CONTENTS.

—◆—

	PAGE
INTRODUCTORY	5
Freshwater Fisheries	6
COMMON LAW PRINCIPLES	7
EARLY ATTEMPTS AT REGULATION	10
SALMON FISHERY ACTS	12
FREE PASSAGE OF FISH	13
RESTRICTIONS ON WEIRS	15
FISH PASSES	17
FIXED ENGINES	19
UNLAWFUL INSTRUMENTS	20
LICENCES	22
POISONING AND POLLUTING RIVERS	23
CLOSE TIMES	24
FRESHWATER FISHERIES ACT, 1878	27
INSPECTORS AND CONSERVATORS	28
CONSTITUTION OF LOCAL BOARDS	29
POWERS OF CONSERVATORS	31
FISHERY DISTRICTS	32
SCOTTISH LAW OF SALMON FISHERIES	33
IRISH LAW	35
Sea Fisheries	36
HERRING AND PILCHARD FISHERIES	37
SCOTTISH HERRING FISHERIES	39
INTERNATIONAL CONVENTIONS	40
CONVENTION WITH FRANCE	40
NORTH SEA CONVENTION	41
OYSTERS AND SHELL-FISH	43
REGULATION OF OYSTER BEDS	44
SEAL FISHERY	46
GENERAL POLICY OF FISHERY LAWS	47

THE FISHERY LAWS.

FISHING takes place either at sea or in rivers or other inland waters. We may thus divide it into sea-fishing and freshwater fishing, though not with strict accuracy of language, as in the latter term we shall have to include fishing in tidal rivers, estuaries, and arms of the sea. There is a wide difference, as everybody knows, between the two kinds of fishing as to their methods and apparatus. The difference is hardly less striking to an Englishman who contemplates them from the legal point of view. Freshwater fisheries are subject to a number of regulations, partly general and partly local, which go into considerable detail, and are not wholly free from obscurity. These regulations are created by Acts of Parliament, or made by persons on whom Parliament has conferred authority for that purpose, and they are naturally a matter of internal or, as we say in technical language, municipal government and jurisdiction. Foreign Powers have nothing to do with them. Sea fisheries, on the other hand, are now but little affected by any purely municipal law or legislation. Whales and sturgeon, and, some books say, other "great fish" caught in English waters belong by ancient prerogative to the Crown. In Scotland the herring fishery has been fostered and regulated by statutes, of which, however, only a very small part remains in force. British subjects fishing in certain parts of the high seas may come under the operation of particular conventions with foreign Powers made by the British Government and confirmed by Parliament. There are also special provisions as to oyster fisheries and other shell-fish. Apart from these, and from any particular convention of the kind just mentioned, there is nothing to prevent any British subject from fishing on the high seas when, where, and how he thinks fit. In territorial waters within the jurisdiction of any foreign State he is subject to the local laws and regulations, whatever they may be. There have been controversies about the extent of a maritime State's jurisdiction in its own coast waters, but it seems to have always been admitted that it includes the regulation of fisheries. Territorial or, as they are sometimes called, marginal waters are commonly understood to extend to a distance of a marine league (three geographical miles) from the shore. This measure, fixed long ago with reference to the supposed extreme range of cannon planted on the land, is thought by some modern authorities to be too short: the question, however, is one of general international law, which cannot be discussed here. For the purpose of fishery rights the three-mile limit is expressly adopted in our conventions with France and other Powers.

A. *Freshwater Fisheries.*

Let us begin at home with the law of freshwater fisheries. The questions with which it deals fall under the two general heads of who may fish, and how they may fish; or, to put the questions as an individual fisherman might put them to himself: May I fish here at all? and, if so, on what conditions and within what limits as to manner, time and otherwise? Restrictions, again, where they exist, may be of two classes; they may be (as most of them are) designed for the preservation of the fish and the benefit of the public, or they may be for the benefit of persons having special rights in that particular fishery. We will take the general question of persons first. Are there any inland waters where all the world are legally entitled to fish? There are certainly some. It is allowed without question that fishing is of common right in the tidal part of an ancient navigable river, unless a contrary private right can be shown. If an exclusive right exists in such water, it is an exception to the common rule of law. It may exist, however, by a grant from the Crown before the date of Magna Charta ; and ancient and continuous usage may establish a judicial presumption that the usage had its legal origin in some such grant. Since Magna Charta the Crown has had no power to make a grant of this kind. Therefore anybody may fish in the Thames below Teddington Lock, for instance, without lawful hindrance except from the person, if any, who can make out his title by special grant or usage to exclusive fishing-rights in the river at the particular spot.[1] In the case of the tidal part of the Thames there are not in fact, so far as I am aware, any such exceptional rights. If we go above Teddington Lock, we find a very different state of things. In practice all manner of people fish on the upper reaches of the Thames and other navigable rivers without interruption. And whether they are within their legal rights in so doing is a question that has been settled in England—and perhaps not finally—only by decisions given so lately as last year.[2] It was long uncertain whether there did or did not exist a public right to fish in navigable rivers above the limits of the tide. In Ireland it has been

---

[1] But not when or as he pleases, for the Thames fisheries are regulated by the Conservators under special statutory powers.

[2] *Pearce* v. *Scotcher*, 9 Q. B. D. 162 (March 31, 1882); *Reece* v. *Miller*, 8 Q. B. D. 626 (April 4, 1882).

held (in 1868)[1] that there is no such right; this decision, though not in itself binding on English, still less on Scottish tribunals, has now been followed in England, and would not improbably be followed in Scotland. The prevailing opinion in the United States is that both the bed of the river and the right of fishing belong to the riparian owners. Even if a public right of fishing did exist, still it would not include or carry as a consequence any right to use the banks of the river for fishing. The bank belongs to the owner of the adjacent ground, and he is no more bound to let strangers come on it to fish than for any other purpose. And if there is a public right of way along the bank—a towing-path, for example—that does not strictly entitle any one to stand there and fish. The land and the power of controlling its use belong to the landowner, subject only to his duty to allow the road or path to be used for the kind of traffic to which it is appropriated. A loiterer on a high road is, strictly speaking, a trespasser; and one who loiters or stops to fish is in no better case. The inhabitants of a particular place on a river-side might possibly have a customary right to fish from the bank, or to use it for drying nets; but such a right, if it could or did exist, would make no difference to the position of a stranger. In Scotland, however, a right to use the bank seems to be more easily allowed than in England when once the right to take fish is established. It must be added that, where public rights of both fishing and navigation exist in the same waters, the fisherman must give way to the merchant sailor in case of need, navigation being deemed of greater public importance than fishing.

[1] A contrary opinion seems to have been entertained by the Court of Queen's Bench in England in the same year; but the point was not before them for argument or decision.

Apart from the case of tidal waters, the general rule is that the fish in inland waters, or more exactly the exclusive right of taking them while they are there, belongs to the owner of the soil under the water, be it river, lake, or pond. In the case of a river being the boundary between two landowners, the bed of the river on either side of the middle line, and consequently the right of fishing, goes with the adjacent land, unless the owner of the farther bank is able to show that the whole bed of the river belongs to him: a state of things which, though exceptional, may exist by the special terms of an ancient grant or the like. The exclusive right to take fish within certain limits of space is called a several fishery. It is most commonly associated with the ownership or occupation of the land under the water, but it may exist separately from it: thus the landowner may sell or let the right to take fish in his waters, and enable the buyer or lessee to exclude all other persons, himself among them.

If the land surrounding or adjacent to ponds or rivers is let to a tenant by deed, the tenant acquires the right of fishing along with the right of occupation unless the landlord expressly reserves it.

In Scotland salmon fishing is a special privilege of the Crown; the right may be, and constantly has been, granted by the Crown to subjects, but no subject can exercise it without distinctly making out his title. The right to fish for trout (and apparently other freshwater fish) is also said to belong to the Crown in the first instance; but a grant of it as "part and pertinent" of the subjacent or adjacent land seems to be assumed without difficulty in the absence of evidence to the contrary, so that practically, as to fish other than salmon, the rule is the same as in England.

It must not be supposed that (even apart from modern

regulation by Acts of Parliament) the landowner entitled to take fish in an adjacent river can deal with them as his absolute property before they are caught. , His right is to catch them in his own water, and (subject to the doubt about fishery in a navigable river being public) to prevent others from catching them.   But he must not artificially prevent the passage and repassage of the fish between his part of the river and his neighbours' by dams, weirs, or the like contrivances.   He must leave to his neighbours the enjoyment of opportunities equal to his own.   Such was the old law, as it appears by Magna Charta,[1] thus interpreted by Coke : " No owner of the banks of rivers shall so appropriate, or keep the rivers several to him, to defend or bar others either to have passage or fish there," (fish must here be the noun, not verb) " otherwise than they were used in the reign of King Henry II."   Another clause in the Charter purported to abolish fishing-weirs : " Omnes kidelli deponantur de cetero penitus per Tamisiam et Medeweyam et per totam Angliam nisi per costeram maris."[2]   Both branches of the law, however, were soon and extensively disregarded.   A series of later Acts of Parliament for the suppression of weirs shows how difficult it was found to keep the action of riparian owners "regarding only their private and greedy profit"[3] within bounds

---

[1] Cap. 16.   An action by an upper against a lower riparian owner on the Dart, for building a new salmon weir to the prejudice of the older one above it, occurs in the newly printed Year-Book of 11 & 12 Ed. III., p. 468.   (A.D. 1338.)   It is reported only as a precedent of pleading, so the result does not appear.

[2] Cap. 23.

[3] These were the words of Parliament in 1705 : 4 & 5 Anne, c. 8, quoted in the judgment of the Fisheries Commissioners in *Leconfield* v. *Lonsdale*, L. R. 5 C. P. at p. 683, where a full account of the old statutes is given.

compatible with the maintenance of either fishery or navigation. All these laws (which were held to apply only to navigable rivers) are now obsolete or superseded. As regards the subject now in hand, the construction of weirs, as well as the employment of the other devices for taking fish known by the generic name of "fixed engines," is fully dealt with by the more recent statutes.

There were abundance of local statutes besides. One made for the Ouse and Humber in 1531 will serve as well as any other for a specimen. The preamble sets forth that "now of late, certain persons studying only for their own private lucre, not regarding the common weal, but daily imagining the utter destruction, ruin and decay" of the city of York and adjoining riparian country, "have and daily do keep, preserve, and maintain certain engines for taking of fish in the said river and water of Ouse and Humber, commonly called Fishgarths; and set in the said river and water, in such places of the same where ships should have their liberal and direct passage, in the midst of the streams of the said river of Ouse and water of Humber, stakes, piles and other things; by reason whereof," not only navigation is endangered, "but also the brood and fry of fish in the said river and water of Ouse and Humber be commonly thereby destroyed and putrified, to the utter impoverishment and destruction of the said city, unless speedy remedy be in this behalf shortly provided." Parliament, moved by this lamentable complaint, provided for the abatement of the fishgarths and piles, and the regulation of fishing in the future.[1]

A similar course of legislation, beginning about the same time or somewhat earlier, took place in Scotland.

We now come to the restrictions created by modern Acts

[1] 23 Hen. 8, c. 18.

of Parliament. These Acts extend over a space of seventeen years, from 1861 to 1878. Every one of them, after the first, refers to its predecessors, and in various ways modifies parts of them. Every separate Act also deals with many distinct branches of the subject, or fragments of such branches. No authoritative consolidation has ever been undertaken, and the state of the law on any given point can be ascertained only by collating and piecing together all the clauses of the several Acts which have any bearing upon it. The provisions of the Acts are also heterogeneous in respect of their extent, both as to the subject-matter and as to local application. Some deal with salmon only, some with specified fish other than salmon, and others with river fish generally. Some of those which deal with fish other than salmon are nevertheless applicable only to salmon rivers. Sometimes parts of different Acts deal with the same matter in such terms that it is by no means easy to say whether the later enactment was or was not intended to supersede the earlier. Many details are left to be filled in or varied at the discretion of the central or local executive authorities. The result of such a condition of things (which is in no way peculiar to the Fishery Acts, but is the normal condition of English statute law) is that it is difficult to obtain a connected view of the effect of existing legislation as a whole, and still more difficult to communicate it accurately to others, especially when those others are understood to be likely to take the exposition on trust. It may be useful to mention that a consolidated reprint of the Salmon Fishery Acts, with proposed amendments, was prepared by Mr. Spencer Walpole, and may be found in the annual report of the Inspectors for 1878, presented to Parliament and published in 1879.

The regulations of the Fishery Acts are chiefly for the preservation of the fish, and in the interest of the public. A few statutory provisions in these Acts and elsewhere are for the protection of the owners of private fisheries. Those which are made in the public interest may be divided into the following classes :—

1. Securities for free passage of migratory fish up and down rivers.

2. Restrictions on modes of fishing.

3. Restrictions on times of fishing.

4. Constitution of authorities, and administrative rules and powers.

Or we may sum up these classes still more shortly under catchwords, thus : Weirs—Foul fishing—Close times—Conservators.

1. *As to free passage of fish.*

This is, as above said, an ancient head of the law, though the old laws, not so much because they were defective in themselves as for want of adequate means of enforcing them, did very little good. To understand the meaning and operation of the rules contained in the Fishery Acts we must have before us the general nature of the facts which have made them necessary. For this purpose we cannot do better than adopt the language used by the Fishery Commissioners [1] in 1870 :—

" Nearly all the great rivers of England are frequented by salmon, a species of migratory fish which can only exist by alternately living in salt and fresh water. The law of their nature is that the fish are bred in the upper and shallow waters of the great rivers and their tributaries, and at the age of about eighteen months they pass down

---

[1] The judgment was prepared by Mr. James Paterson.

to the sea, and the rest of their existence is spent in passing
every year to and fro between the sea and the upper fresh
streams. At all times of the year the fish are either
passing up or passing down the river. It is true the
greater numbers pass up in the summer months, but there
are generally some passing up or going down at other times
also. They are not bred at all, and cannot be bred, in
the tidal parts of rivers, though there they are caught
plentifully.

"To enable the fish to inhabit a river, that is to say, to be
found not only in the fresh but the tidal parts of rivers, it is
thus essential that the parent fish should have an open
passage from the sea to the source, or at least to the upper
shallows of the river. The old fish require to go up the river
to breed, and the young fish require to come down the river
to grow; and after they are grown they still require to
alternate between the fresh waters and the sea. If at any
point between the tidal limit and the upper breeding-
grounds a barrier is made which obstructs this passage,
the stock of fish is necessarily diminished and gradually
annihilated. It thus follows that at the place where the
salt water meets the fresh, the whole stock of fish of the
river and estuary must pass at least once in their lives,
either coming or going. This is so in a state of nature,
irrespective of all laws. If all the fish must pass a particular spot, it equally follows that they may all with
certainty be caught at that spot if certain obvious means
for that end are used.

"A weir is, in general terms, a kind of fixed structure
stretching across a river, the sole object of which is to make
a barrier to the progress of the fish, and so to compel
them into certain places or apertures, in which traps,
boxes, cruives, or coops are set, which confine and catch

the fish. This barrier, which may or may not extend across the whole breadth of the river, is either of solid masonry or of brushwood, or it may be of any substance and texture sufficiently high and closely reticulated to stop the fish, and lead them into the apertures which contain the boxes or traps." [1]

. A mill-dam or mill-weir, though its purpose is only to dam up and collect the water above it for the use of the mill, may have and often has, according to its width and height, the same effect in stopping the passage of fish. There are also mill-dams with which a fishing-weir is purposely combined as part of the same structure. These are called in the Acts fishing mill-dams.

It is easily seen that if there were no check on the maintenance and use of weirs and dams, it would be in the power of a few persons to monopolise and ultimately destroy the whole fish stock of our rivers, or at any rate the migratory species. Other riparian owners, indeed, might without the aid of Parliament complain of the infringement of their rights of fishery; but the difficulty of proving substantial damage in particular cases, and the still greater difficulty of combined action, make the common-law rights of private owners all but nugatory. Hence the statutory regulation which has been undertaken.

In England the general rules are now in substance as follows :

It is unlawful to take salmon by means of a dam or weir,[2] unless it is constructed for the sole purpose of catching fish, or partly to catch fish and partly as a

[1] *Leconfield* v. *Lonsdale*, L. R. 5 C. P. 664, 666.

[2] " Fishing weir" in the Acts means " any erection, structure, or obstruction fixed to the soil either temporarily or permanently across, or partly across, a river or branch of a river, and which is used for the

mill-dam, and was lawfully in use, under a grant or otherwise, before 1861.[1]

The penalties are fines which may go up to £5 for each offence, and £1 besides for every salmon caught; and both the fish and the traps and tackle used in catching them are to be forfeited. For a second offence against any of the provisions of the Acts half the full penalty must be imposed, and for a third offence the whole; except where the full penalty exceeds £5, in which cases 50s. is allowed to stand as the minimum penalty for a second offence, and £5 for a third.[2]

If a fishing weir extends more than half-way across the stream at its lowest state of water,[3] it must have a free gap for the passage of fish in the deepest part of the weir stream, as deep as the natural bed, and one-tenth part as wide as the stream, within the limits of three feet, the least width allowed, and forty, the greatest that can be required in any case. A fishing mill-dam,[4] of whatever size, must have a fish pass of a pattern approved by the Home Office (the authority in which the general superintendence of the Salmon Fisheries is vested)[5] with

exclusive purpose of catching or facilitating the catching of fish," Salmon Fishery Act, 1873, s. 4. Salmon includes "all migratory fish of the genus Salmon," by whatever local name known. A long list of such names is given, 1861, s. 4. In following notes the Acts will be cited, as now, by their dates alone.

[1] The terms of the Act (1861, s. 12) are narrower, but have been interpreted to include any form of lawful title.

[2] 1865, s. 57, as varied by 1873, s. 18, sub-s. 5.

[3] 1861, s. 12, as held in *Rolle* v. *Whyte*, L. R. 3 Q. B. 286, to be limited by s. 27.

[4] 1861, s. 12. "Such pass shall not be larger nor deeper than requisite for the above purposes;" I suppose this means "need not."

[5] 1861, s. 31. In this Act (but not in the later ones) the term "Home Office" is used, through the machinery of a definition clause,

enough water to enable salmon to use it. The consequence of neglecting these directions is that the weir or dam, though lawful as far as antiquity goes, is regarded as an unlawful one, and the penalties above mentioned are incurred by using it for salmon fishing.

All fishing for salmon otherwise than with rod and line in the immediate neighbourhood of a weir or dam (50 yards above, 100 yards below), or in a mill-race or weir cut, is illegal; and so is fishing in the like places, even with rod and line, "in such a manner as to wilfully scare or hinder salmon" from passing in the usual manner. The penalties are the same as for using an unlawful weir or dam; but if the weir or dam is provided with a proper fish pass, the person entitled to the local right of fishing must be compensated before they can be enforced.[1]

It is also forbidden under similar penalties to "place any device for the purpose of obstructing the passage of the young of salmon."[2]

The Acts contain various directions as to making fis passes and "free gaps," of which the general effect is that the owner of an old dam, subject to the discretion of the local conservators and the Home Office, is liable to have a fish pass made in it (but is entitled on application within two years to compensation, if his dam is injured thereby), and the constructor of a new dam, and the owner

---

instead of "One of Her Majesty's Principal Secretaries of State," which is the proper legal expression—the assignment of particular duties to a particular Secretary of State under the name of the Home Office being a matter of administrative convenience, and no part of the Constitution as recognised by positive law.

[1] 1873, s. 17, extending and apparently superseding the provisions of 1861, s. 12, sub-s. 2, which, however, is not repealed.

[2] 1861, s. 15.

C

of every fishing weir, is absolutely bound under penalties to keep a sufficient pass or gap, and if there is not one already, to make one ;[1] failing which, the Home Office may have the work done at his expense.[2] These latter rules apply to the rebuilding or restoring of old weirs or dams, and to all artificial obstructions to the passage of salmon.[3]

Injuring or obstructing fish passes is an offence punishable with fine up to £5, the expense of reinstatement, and, if the injury is a continuing one, a further daily fine up to £1 for so long as it is continued.[4]

In special cases weirs, dams, and the like may be taken by the local conservators by way of compulsory purchase ; but this is an extraordinary proceeding, though it has sometimes been put in use. The conservators must first petition the Home Office ; the Home Secretary, if satisfied that there is a case for inquiry, directs an inquiry, and on the result of this he may make a provisional order for compulsory purchase, which must be confirmed by an Act of Parliament in order to take effect.[5] But if the conservators can come to an agreement with the owner of a weir, &c., they may, at their own discretion, buy it for the purpose of removal.[6]

Owners of artificial cuts leading out of salmon rivers must provide gratings to keep young salmon from coming down them,[7] and local conservators also have power to fix gratings for the same purpose, provided that they do not hinder navigation or other rights to the use of the water.[8]

By the Act of 1865 the function of inquiring into

---

[1] 1861, ss. 23–25, 28 ; 1865, s. 32.   [2] 1873, s. 46.
[3] 1873, s. 48.   [4] 1873, s. 49.
[5] 1865, s. 27, sub-s. (3).   [6] 1861, s. 13.
[7] 1873, ss. 58–61.

the legality of fishing weirs, and causing illegal ones to be abated, was conferred on certain Special Commissioners, whose office (as having fully performed its purposes) was abolished in 1873.[1]

2. *As to modes of fishing.*

Closely connected with the use of weirs to take salmon is the use of "fixed engines," that is, nets or other contrivances fixed to the bed or banks of a river, or in any way set in the river, so to speak, as a trap, for the purpose of catching fish or assisting in their capture. Evidently the prohibition of taking fish by weirs would lose much of its effect if they might be taken by other self-acting devices permanently set in the river, though not amounting, like a continuous weir, to a total obstruction of the fish's passage. Indeed, a fishing weir may be described as only the most complete and therefore most mischievous form of fixed engine, though for legal purposes it is not covered by that term. The other means that can be used are various; the chief of them are specified in the definition clause of the Act of 1861, by which "fixed engine" is made to include, for the purposes of the Act, "stake-nets, bag-nets, putts, putchers,[2] and all fixed implements or engines for catching or for facilitating the catching of fish." The Act of 1865 (s. 39) extended the term to "include any net or other imple-

---

[1] 36 Vict. c. 13.

[2] Putts and putchers are large conical basket-traps for fish, something like a much elongated lobster-pot. The legal reader may be referred to L. R. 3 Q. B. 156, 643, for information as to their structure : there is also an account of them in Mr. Buckland's evidence before the Select Committee of 1869, and specimens are shown in the Exhibition by the Severn Fisheries Board. They are used only in the estuary of the Severn.

ment for taking fish fixed to the soil, or made stationary
in any other way, not being a fishing weir or fishing mill-
dam;" and a still further extension was made in 1873,
(s. 4), so as to include floating nets and tackle.

No fixed engine may be used except such as in 1861,
or one of the four preceding seasons, were in lawful use,
(that is, were used under a title, by grant or otherwise, which
would have afforded a good answer to any objection by
neighbouring fishery owners on the ground of interference
with their rights.)[1]   The prohibition extends to the use of
fixed engines as merely auxiliary to the taking of salmon,
or for obstructing their passage.[2]   If it is infringed, the
engine and any salmon taken are forfeited, and there is a fine
which may go up to £10 for every day's use of the illegal
instrument.   The Fishery Commissioners, while their office
existed, had power to determine what fixed engines should
be "privileged" as having been lawfully in use in 1861 or
earlier as above mentioned; on the other hand they were
charged with the duty of inquiring into the legality or
otherwise of fixed engines, and were empowered to order
the removal of illegal ones.[3]   Moreover it has been
judicially decided that an illegal fixed engine, like any
other nuisance, may lawfully be removed by any of the
Queen's subjects.   Practically no one but a conservator or
some one under his orders is likely to do this; the important application of the doctrine is to protect (as it did in
the case in question) a conservator who, whether by zeal
or inadvertence, acts outside his own district.

Divers other modes of fishing are prohibited with a view
to the preservation of salmon and (through the extensions
introduced in the later Acts) other freshwater fish also.

[1] 1851, s. 11, as amended by 1865, s. 39.   [2] 1873, s. 18.
[3] 1865, ss. 42–45.

Lights must not be used for catching salmon, neither must snares, spears and similar instruments (but a gaff may be used as an auxiliary to angling, except at seasons when it is forbidden by the local conservators).[1] The use of "otters" is also forbidden.[2] Fish roe must not be used as bait, or bought or sold; and even the possession of it, except for scientific purposes, and with the consent in writing of the conservators in a district for which a board of conservators is established,[3] is unlawful.[4] These prohibitions apply to fishing for trout and char within the limits of any fishery district for which there are conservators,[5] and everywhere else in England, except in the counties of Norfolk and Suffolk and the city of Norwich,[6] where the fisheries are regulated by a special Board of Conservators under a local Act of 1877.[7] The penalties are fines up to a maximum of £5, and forfeiture of illegal instruments; on a third conviction, imprisonment with hard labour up to six months may be inflicted, and on a second conviction, the offender's fishing licence, if he has one, must be forfeited.[8]

Net fishing is allowed (subject to the restrictions mentioned under the foregoing head in the neighbourhood of weirs) only on condition of the meshes being of certain minimum dimensions,[9] and a seine or draft net must not be shot within 100 yards of the line of shot of another

---

[1] 1873, s. 39, sub-s. (9).

[2] 1873, s. 18. An "otter" is a piece of wood used for running out baits.   [3] 1865, s. 60.

[4] 1861, ss. 8, 9.   [5] 1865, s. 64.

[6] Freshwater Fisheries Act, 1878, ss. 3 and 5.

[7] 40 & 41 Vict. c. xcviii.   [8] 1865, s. 56.

[9] "Two inches in extension from knot to knot (the measurement to be made on each side of the square) or eight inches measured round each mesh when wet:" 1861, s. 10; but by 1873, s. 39, conservators may fix the minimum lawful size between the limits of 1½ and 2½ inches.

which is being already worked, until that other is drawn in and landed.[1] Fine up to £5 is the penalty for breaking either of these rules. The use of nets may be regulated in various other ways, and net fishing at night, except for eels, prohibited altogether, under local by-laws made by conservators.[2]

Further, no salmon fishing of any kind may be carried on in a fishery district without a licence, on pain of fines which (as far as I can make out from the different provisions of two Acts) may amount to £20 for using any unlicensed instrument other than rod and line "for catching salmon," and £5 for assisting in such use, or fishing for salmon with any such instrument; or killing them with any such instrument without actually catching them; or taking or killing them, or attempting so to do, without any instrument at all. In the case of the unlicensed angler or user of an instrument, the penalty must not be less than double licence duty. There is a distinct penalty up to £1 for every salmon caught.[3]

The money paid for licences goes to defray the expenses of administering the Acts.[4] Local boards of conservators now have power to extend the licensing system to trout and char as well as salmon fishing, if they think fit.[5]

Against the wholesale destruction of fish, whether by design or by negligent pollution of rivers, there are special pro-

---

[1] 1873, s. 14.   [2] 1873, s. 39.

[3] 1865, ss. 35, 36; 1873, s. 22, which purports not to affect the former enactments, in other words, makes a Chinese puzzle of them by leaving it as uncertain as possible what addition to the law was really intended. I suppose it was thought doubtful whether the offence of using an unlicensed instrument "for catching salmon" would be committed if none were in fact caught; if so, the fear was groundless (see *Ruther* v. *Harris*, 1 Ex. D. 97).

[4] 1865, s. 33.   [5] 1878, s. 7.

visions. Dynamite or other explosives must not be used
to catch or destroy fish in a public fishery in any part of the
United Kingdom, or in the adjacent seas within a marine
league of the coast, nor in a private fishery in England, on
pain of fine up to £20 or imprisonment, which may be with
hard labour, up to two months.[1] The poisoning of any salmon
rivers,[2] as well as of any waters where there is a private right
of fishery,[3] with "any lime or other noxious material," in
order to destroy fish, is an offence punishable with penal
servitude up to seven years. Pollution of salmon rivers
"to such an extent as to cause the waters to poison or kill
fish" (though not intended to have that effect) is punishable by fine on an increasing scale, ending in £20 a day
after a third conviction. But the party may escape
these penalties, if his act in sending refuse, or whatever it
may be, into the river, is not otherwise unlawful[4] and he
can show that, being thus in the exercise of his right, "he
has used the best practicable means, within a reasonable
cost, to render harmless the liquid or solid matter so
permitted to flow or to be put into [5] waters." Probably
it is not difficult to satisfy justices of this in a manufacturing district; again, if the stuff poured into the river is so
noxious that there are not any practicable means at all of
rendering it harmless, it is by no means clear whether any
penalty is incurred.[6] The person complained of may also,
if a decision against him would cost him more than £100,

---

[1] 1878, s. 32.   [2] 1873, s. 13.

[3] 24 & 25 Vict. c. 97, s. 32. It has been suggested that this would
apply to acts done by an owner of strictly private waters (ponds or the
like) on his own land; but I do not think it will bear such a construction.

[4] It might be unlawful, for example, as amounting to a public
nuisance, or being forbidden by a local Act.

[5] The wearisome but inevitable "such" of accustomed parliamentary
style appears to have dropped out of the text.   [6] 1861, s. 5.

require an action to be brought in the High Court of Justice to settle the question whether he has used the "best practicable means," and it is not hard to guess what, on such a question, the bias of jurymen in a manufacturing country is likely to be. Altogether, this enactment has the air of belonging to the family, well known to English lawyers and administrators, of excellent commands of the legislature so cunningly and tenderly fenced about with safeguards for the liberty of the subject that in practice nobody minds them. For whatever reason, the pollution of rivers has in fact not ceased, and it is by no means confined to the manufacturing districts. In the mining country of the West of England it not infrequently happens that an abandoned mine is started afresh for merely speculative purposes, the foul water of the old workings pumped out into the nearest river, and the fish destroyed, without the conservators being practically able to apply any remedy. Should they not have power in such cases to issue an injunction and stop the mischief beforehand ? The power of entering which may now be exercised on a magistrate's order,[1] or a special order of the conservators,[2] is hardly enough.

3. *As to close times.*

This class of regulations is designed to prevent fish from being recklessly taken during their periods of breeding and migration so as to destroy the stock for future seasons.

Young salmon must not be taken or destroyed, bought or sold, or kept in any one's possession, except for artificial propagation or other scientific purposes. A like rule applies to "unclean or unseasonable"[3] salmon, trout, and

---

[1] 1865, s. 31.   [2] 1873, s. 37.

[3] "Unseasonable salmon seem to be all salmon out of season, that is, all salmon taken during the annual close time. Unclean salmon would seem to be salmon unfit to be taken, wherever and whenever

char, and the mere attempt to take them is also punishable. The punishments are fine up to £5, and separate fines up to £1 for each fish unlawfully dealt with, and on a third conviction imprisonment up to six months (which may be with hard labour) at the discretion of the court.[1] There is an exception in favour of scientific purposes, and it is provided (perhaps superfluously) that a fisherman taking unseasonable fish by accident incurs no penalty if he forthwith puts them back in the water. It has also been judicially decided that it is not an offence under the Acts to catch young salmon in fishing for trout, and keep them in the mistaken belief that they are trout.

All salmon fishing is prohibited between the 1st of November and the 1st of February; between the 1st of September and the 1st of November angling, but no other kind of fishing, is allowed.[2] The close time may be varied by the local conservators, but must begin not later than the 1st of November for nets, or the 1st of December for rods.[3] For putts and putchers a longer close time is fixed without power of variation, from September 1st to May 1st inclusive.[4] There are similar provisions as to trout and char,[5] with similar power to the conservators to vary the close time within the limits of September 2 and November 2 for its beginning:[6] if they do not fix it by any by-law, the close time is from October 2 to

---

caught, even if during the open season; thus a kelt would be an unclean salmon, a clean run fish caught in December an unseasonable fish." Willis Bund, Law of Salmon Fisheries, p. 336.

[1] 1861, ss. 14, 15; 1873, s. 18, sub-ss. (3) and (8); and (as to penalties) 1865, s. 56. [2] 1861, s. 17.

[3] 1873, s. 39, (1). [4] 1879 (42 & 43 Vict. c. 26).

[5] 1865, s. 64, extended to char, 1873, s. 18, (7), and to all English waters, whether salmon rivers or not, by the Freshwater Fisheries Act, 1878. [6] 1876 (39 & 40 Vict. c. 19); 1878, s. 10.

February 1. As to salmon there is also, during the fishing season, a weekly close time for net fishing, generally from noon on Saturday till six on Monday morning, but conservators can vary it within limits.[1] The penalties are similar to those already mentioned for fishing with illegal instruments. During the annual close season fixed engines must be removed altogether, and during the weekly close season a free passage must be left through them.[2]

Penalties are likewise imposed on selling fish in the close season, and the exportation of unseasonable salmon between the 3rd of September and the 30th of April is specially provided against.[3] As to trout and char it has fallen out in the complication of additions and minor amending Acts that there is no power to vary the time during which they may be lawfully sold; so that in districts where the close time for capture has been varied absurd results may follow. It may be an offence to sell fish while it is still lawful to catch them, and while it is still unlawful to catch them they may be sold with impunity.

As an additional protection to salmon rivers, eel-pots and the like, except eel-baskets used with bait, not more than ten inches across, and not at a dam or weir, must not be set in them between the 1st of January and the 24th of June,[4] and during the same time "any device whatsoever to catch or obstruct any fish descending the stream," is unlawful in any inland water, whether frequented by salmon or not.

In 1878 a new close season (March 15 to June 15 in-

[1] 1861, s. 21 ; 1873, s. 39, (2).   [2] 1861, ss. 20, 22.
[3] 1865, s. 65 ; 33 & 34 Vict. c. 33.
[4] 1873, s. 15 (but elvers may be taken at any time, subject to certain special close times for the Severn Fishery : 39 & 40 Vict. c. 34.) This extends to the use of a permanent eel-trap, which existed before the passing of the Act : *Briggs* v. *Swanwick*, 10 Q. B. D. 510.

clusive) was established for freshwater fish in general, not being migratory fish,[1] or pollan, trout or char, on pain of fine up to forty shillings. But the owner of a private fishery, or the conservators of a public one, may dispense with this prohibition as to angling; and the owner of a private fishery "where trout, char, or grayling are specially preserved" may keep down the inferior fish.[2] Conservators have a further power of generally exempting their district with the approval of the Home Secretary. Altogether the exceptions are so large that they seem to leave but little room for the operation of the rule. The majority of freshwater fisheries are private, and as nobody knows exactly what is meant by "specially preserving" trout, &c., the owner of a private fishery has only to say that he preserves the trout in order to go on doing as he pleases.

Notwithstanding its defects both of form and of substance, however, the Act of 1878 has on some rivers done much good in the hands of willing and able conservators. The key to its policy, which is not evident from the text itself, appears to be furnished by the late Mr. Buckland's evidence when the Bill was before a Select Committee. His doctrine was that the main point was to establish a close time for nets; and that it was desirable to be very indulgent to angling, that it might be the interest of anglers to assist in enforcing the law.

As early as 1558 an attempt was made for the general

---

[1] "Those kinds which migrate to or from the open sea." These words raise troublesome questions of natural history; as to eels, for instance. Probably the framers of the Act were thinking only of salmon and sea-trout.

[2] 1878, s. 11. Does this include an occupier who has the general right of fishing?

protection of freshwater fisheries (" An Act for Preservation of Spawn and Fry of Fish," 1 Eliz. c. 17). It does not appear that this Act, except as to salmon, has ever been expressly repealed ; its provisions are wider than those of the Freshwater Fisheries Act, 1878, but I am not aware that they have been enforced in recent times. The Act of 1861 repeals the Act of Elizabeth (originally a temporary one) so far as relates to salmon, and then repeals without qualification an Act of Charles I. which made it perpetual. The legal effect of this is not very clear.

4. *As to local Authorities and Administration.*

The first of the modern Salmon Fisheries Acts, that of 1861, left the enforcement of its provisions to the County Sessions under the general direction of the Home Office. This direction was to be exercised by two inspectors, for whose appointment the Act gives authority. At present the only inspector is Mr. Huxley, and it is not intended to fill up the vacant place. By the same Act the justices had power to appoint conservators, but no provision was made either for expenses or for the co-operation of the conservators of different counties traversed or washed by the same salmon river. In consequence of these grave omissions [1] the Act of 1865 provided for the creation of Fishery Districts. The Home Office was empowered to make a fishery district including the whole of any salmon river, on an application from the justices of any of its riparian counties. [2] The Home Secretary may alter fishery districts [3] on the application of the conservators. In 1873

[1] 1865, preamble.   [2] 1865, s. 4, &c.

[3] 1873, s. 5, &c. A list of the fishery districts constituted in England and Wales down to 1878, and of the variations of close times, &c., adopted in many of them, may be seen in Oke's Handy Book of the

the constitution of boards of conservators was varied by adding a representative element in certain cases, and in 1878 the provisions of the former Acts were extended to trout as well as salmon rivers.

By the combined effect of these Acts, the constitution of boards of conservators is shortly as follows. There are three classes of members :

1. Members appointed by the justices in quarter sessions. In the case of a fishery district extending into two or more counties, the process was this : the justices in the several quarter sessions appointed fishery committees, who together formed a joint fishery committee for the district and appointed conservators and regulated various incidental matters, after which the committee was dissolved.[1] The conservators hold office for one year ; after the first year the appointments are made by the several counties in the proportions which have been fixed by the original joint committee. The like proceedings would still have to be taken for the formation of a new fishery district not wholly in one county.

In the case of estuaries formed by the union of more than one salmon river, the Home Secretary may assign the jurisdiction over it to one or more of the local boards of conservators, or form a special combined board :[2] but this provision has not been found of much use.

2. *Ex officio* members. The owner or occupier of every fishery in the district of the rateable annual value of £30,

---

Fishery Laws, ed. Willis Bund, London, 1878. The map in the 18th Report of the Inspectors (1879) shows the districts at a glance. But any one wanting to know the rules in force at any place for practical purposes should by no means omit to obtain the latest information on the spot.

[1] 1865, ss. 7–13.   [2] 1865, s. 19.

and every landowner having in the district at least a mile of riparian frontage on either or both sides of a salmon or trout river, and the right of fishery therein, and having paid licence duty for the last season, is an *ex officio* member of the board of conservators for the district.[1] He is required to declare his qualification before acting on the board.[2]

3. Representative members. In a district where there is any public or common fishery, those persons who exercise the right of fishing therein, and have taken out licences for net fishing for salmon, are entitled to elect one member to the board for every £50 of licence duty paid by them.[3] The election is by plural voting according to the amount of duty paid by the elector, and the voting is also cumulative : the voting papers must be attested, and may be sent in by post.[4] Elections are held yearly, and it is the business of the board of conservators to ascertain the persons entitled to be electors and give them notice of their rights.[5]

These provisions seem practically to apply only to the sea-coast and tidal waters ; for there are few if any public fisheries anywhere else. As to common rights of fishing (as distinguished from public) the tenants of an inland manor may no doubt be entitled to fish in the lord's waters within it, and such a right is known to the law as common of fishery. I do not know, however, that it is frequent or important in practice ; and I rather doubt whether any

[1] 1873, s. 26 : (extended to " any river frequented by salmon, trout, or char," 1878, s. 6). Provision is made for the representation of persons under disability by s. 27.　　　[2] 1873, s. 28.

[3] 1873, s. 29. The Act does not say that the public or common fishery must be a salmon fishery.

[4] The Act says the voter " *shall* send the voting paper by post to the returning officer," &c., but I suppose a voting paper delivered by the voter in person would be good.　　　[5] S. 30.

definite meaning was attached by Parliament to the term "common rights of fishing" which is used in the Act.

A Board of Conservators, being duly constituted, may appoint water bailiffs, issue fishing licences, acquire dams, weirs, and fixed engines for the purpose of removing them, take . legal proceedings against offending persons, and generally supervise and protect the fisheries in their district,[1] and expend funds in their hands in the improvement of them in any lawful manner.[2] Water-bailiffs appointed by the conservators have extensive powers of search, and the same privileges and protection as constables in the execution of their office.[3] They may also, with special authority from a magistrate or the conservators, enter on private grounds to detect or prevent breaches of the law.[4] Any one authorised in writing by the conservators may also enter upon lands to inspect weirs and other obstructions.[5] Conservators may also make by-laws as to sundry matters of detail (which for the most part have been incidentally mentioned in their places), subject to confirmation by the Home Office.[6] The by-laws must be printed and published, and every one taking out a fishing-licence is entitled to a copy.[7]

Penalties under the Salmon Fishery Acts are enforceable by proceedings before Justices according to the directions of the Summary Jurisdiction Acts.[8] Besides these general Acts, there are special Acts of Parliament regulating the fisheries of divers rivers and districts; the chief rivers

[1] 1865, s. 27; as to the conditions of licences, 1873, ss. 21, 24, 25, 57.
[2] 1873, s. 23.　　　　　　　　　　　　[3] 1873, s. 36.
[4] 1865, s. 31; 1873, s. 37.　　　　　[5] 1873, s. 56.
[6] 1873, s. 39, &c.　　　　　　　　　[7] 1873, s. 43.
[8] 1873, s. 62.

subject to special rules are the Thames[1] and the Severn.   In a summary account like the present it is of course impossible to go into these matters ; the working of local rules, for the rest, is useful to be known only where they are in force, and is better ascertained there than anywhere else.   It may be just worth while to mention that the rules of the Thames Conservancy as to close times extend to all river fish— including eels, though not by name, as the Court of Common Pleas decided in 1871.   Almost all the rivers of any importance in England are now either included in fishery districts or under special local Acts.   The chief exceptions are in the north the Derwent of Cumberland, and in the south the Itchen.   Others are in the north-west the Mersey, long since hopelessly destroyed as a fish river, and in the east the Witham, Welland and Great Ouse, which have never been salmon rivers at all.   Roughly speaking, a line following the valleys of the Trent and the three several Avons of Gloucestershire, Somersetshire and Hants, will leave to its north and west the part of England where fishery districts are the rule, to the south and east that where they are the exception.

Thus much as to the laws for the general protection of inland fisheries in England.   A few enactments give particular protection or remedies to the owners of private fisheries against trespassers.   Taking fish unlawfully in private waters is a misdemeanour punishable by fine, and a trespassing fisherman's rod, net or other tackle may be seized by the owner of the land or fishery ; but an angler against whom this right is exercised in the day-time escapes any further penalty.[2]   There used to be in

---

[1] The Thames Conservators, I need hardly add, are charged with a number of matters of public interest, of which fishery regulation is only one.   [2] 24 & 25 Vict. c. 96, ss. 24, 25.

the annual Mutiny Act an odd clause for the better preservation of game and fish in places where officers were quartered, it being supposed, apparently, that officers were more likely than other persons to take game and fish without leave. This was dropped in the general revision of military law which took place in 1879 and 1881, presumably because the security of the ordinary law is now enough.

5. *Law of Scotland as to Freshwater Fisheries.*

Scotland is under a system of statutory regulation of the same general kind as the English Acts, which is less complicated and minute, but is pronounced by those who have watched its working to be also less efficient. The leading modern Act on Scotch salmon fisheries was passed in 1862. Under it a board of three Commissioners was formed, with power to fix a district for each river, determine close time, and make other general rules. District boards are elected by the fishery proprietors with voting power according to value, the largest fishery owner in the district being *ex officio* a member and chairman; their functions are more limited and purely ministerial than those of conservators in England.[1] It appears that this system fails to provide good working boards, though in particular cases it may furnish an energetic landowner with useful powers. The Duke of Sutherland, it is stated, constitutes in his own person the district boards for several rivers. In 1868[2] further provisions were made for the appointment and proceedings of district boards, and the Home Office was empowered, on the application of a district

[1] 25 & 26 Vict. c. 97, ss. 18, 22, &c.
[2] 31 & 32 Vict. c. 123.

D

board, to vary the regulations as to close time and otherwise. Fishing in close time,[1] obstructing the passage
of salmon, using illegal instruments, and the like, are
specifically forbidden by the same Act. The prohibitions
and penalties are, as far as they go, so like those of the
English Acts, though they are not identical, that it seems
needless to give them in detail. In the matter of fixed
engines they are a long way behind the English rules,
and grave complaint is still made in Scotland of the
inadequacy of the law as it stands.

The border rivers Tweed and Esk formerly occasioned
much petty contention between the two kingdoms: for
some time the Tweed was carefully excepted from the
rules laid down by Acts of the Scots Parliament, who
thought it hard that if Englishmen were free to pursue
salmon poaching on their own side of the Tweed the
dwellers on the Scottish bank should not have their share.
At present the Tweed is under special statutes of its own,
and the Esk is by the Act of 1865 annexed to England
for the purposes of the Salmon Fishery Acts.

By an Act of last session [2] a Fishery Board was established for Scotland, consisting of three sheriffs selected
and six other members appointed by the Crown. They
have the general superintendence of the salmon fisheries of
Scotland (as well as the herring fishery, of which presently),
and may exercise the powers given by the former Acts to
Commissioners. The Home Office is authorised to appoint

---

[1] There is a curious little reservation in s. 15, sub-s. 2. It is an
offence to fish for salmon during the weekly close time, except *during
Saturday or Monday* by rod and line. We can hardly suppose that
angling on Sunday is thought specially injurious to the fishery at times
of year when it is harmless on Saturday and Monday; the only conclusion therefore seems to be that angling on Sunday is prohibited as
being wicked in itself.   [2] 45 & 46 Vict. c. 78.

an inspector of salmon fisheries for Scotland, who is to work under the Board and report to them.

Trout and other freshwater fish must not be taken in Scottish waters by nets or several other specified means (practically, may be taken only by angling) by any one not having the right of fishery or licensed by the person having it.[1]

Law of Ireland as to Freshwater Fisheries.

Ireland, again, has a separate legislative history, beginning, as far as modern practical purposes are concerned, in the year 1842, when a consolidating Act was passed,[2] and a great number of old Irish statutes as to salmon and other fisheries were repealed. This Act appears to have been to some extent the model for the English Act of 1861. Its provisions are very full and elaborate. In 1848,[3] commissioners and conservators were established and the system of licences introduced; the powers and proceedings of these officers were further defined in 1850.[4] Fresh regulations were introduced (partly, in turn, adopted from the English Act of 1861) by the Salmon Fishery (Ireland) Act, 1863.[5] In 1869[6] the duties of the former Special Commissioners were transferred to inspectors, who now have the power (among other things) of making by-laws, varying local close times, and issuing certificates and licences. They are styled the Inspectors of Irish Fisheries, are three in number, and are appointed by the Lord Lieutenant.[7]

---

[1] 8 & 9 Vict. c. 26, 23 & 24 Vict. c. 45.   [2] 5 & 6 Vict. c. 106.
[3] 11 & 12 Vict. c. 92.   [4] 13 & 14 Vict. c. 88.
[5] 26 & 27 Vict. c. 114.   [6] 32 Vict. c. 9, 32 & 33 Vict. c. 92.
[7] An analysis of the Irish Statutes on the same scale as that above given of the English ones would be wholly beyond my means and

A remarkable feature about the administrative part of the Irish Acts is that the cruisers of the Royal Navy and the coast guard on the sea coast, and the constabulary inland, are specially authorised to enforce their provisions.

B.—SEA FISHERIES.

I. *Generally.*

Of all sea fish the most important to mankind, in our seas at any rate, is the herring. Long ago his pre-eminence among fish was attested in the quaint fancy of the North German tale, which tells how the fish needed a king to maintain order among them, and swam a race for the kingdom ; how the herring surpassed the rest in swiftness, and was proclaimed king, but the sole, angry and envious at being far behind in the race, reviled him, and has been punished by having a wry mouth ever since.[1]

And the legislation of these kingdoms (notably of Scotland) has for centuries endeavoured to protect and foster

---

space. The present account, short as it is, may be of some little use, for the Index to the Revised Statutes (*tit.* Fishery, Ireland) gives nothing but the year and chapter, though the English Acts are pretty fully abstracted.

[1] Die Fische waren schon lange unzufrieden dass keine Ordnung in ihrem Reiche herrschte . . . und vereinigten sich den zu ihrem Herren zu wählen, der am schnellsten die Fluthen durchstreichen und dem Schwachen Hilfe bringen könnte. Sie stellten sich also am Ufer in Reihe und Glied auf, und der Hecht gab mit dem Schwanz ein Zeichen, worauf sie alle zusammen aufbrachen. . . . Auf einmal ertönte der Ruf, " der Hering ist vor ! " der Hering ist vor ! " Wen is vör ? " schrie verdriesslich die platte missgünstige Scholle, die weit zurückgeblieben war, "wen is vör ? " " Der Hering, der Hering " war die Antwort. " De nackte Hiering ? " rief die neidische, " de nackte Hiering ? " Seit der Zeit steht der Scholle zur Strafe das Maul schief.— Grimm, Kinder und Hausmärchen, No. 172. Observe the local colour given by the sole speaking Platt-deutsch.

the herring fisheries in various ways, of which most have been abandoned as contrary to modern commercial policy. Almost the only surviving part of these provisions is the Scotch system of herring branding, which, even if open to some theoretical objections, is found effectual and popular, and has been deliberately maintained. In England the western counties obtained, as long ago as 1604, a wholesome exemption from the strict rights given to landowners by the common law. The statute recites that "the trade of fishing for herrings, pilchards and sean-fish [1] within the counties of Somerset, Devon and Cornwall is, and of late time hath been, very great and profitable"; that "divers persons within the said counties, called balkers, huors, condors, directors, or guidors . . . time out of mind have used to watch and attend upon the high hills and grounds near adjoining to the sea-coasts within the said counties," to watch for the shoals of fish, and give directions to the fishermen, and that landowners have begun to object to their land being entered on for this purpose, and to treat the watchers and fishermen as trespassers; and for the benefit of the fishing trade it enacts that the use of the shore shall be free both to the "watchmen, balkers, huors, condors, directors, and guidors" for their look-out, and to the fishermen for drawing in their nets and landing the fish. [2]

[1] Sean (now commonly written seyn or seine) is a large draw-net. The statute seems applicable chiefly to the pilchard fishery, in which the seine has not lost its importance, though in the herring fishery drift-nets are more commonly used. Drift-net fishing and trawling are now prohibited within two miles of the coast of Cornwall below Trevose Head: Sea Fisheries Act, 1868, s. 68. And by a local Act, 4 & 5 Vict. c. lvii., which regulates the pilchard fishery in St. Ives Bay, a close time (25 July–25 December) for hook fishing, ground fishing, and trawling is established (s. 48) for the space of 1000 fathoms from the shore within the limits of the fishing stations specified by the Act.

[2] 1 Jac. 1, c. 23.

Like rights are given to fishermen everywhere on the Irish coasts by the Irish Fisheries Act of 1842.[1]

In Scotland no legislation of this kind, local or general, was needed; for the common law, by a wiser and more liberal policy than the English, admits the common right to use both the shores of the sea and the banks of public rivers for " white fishing," that is, for catching any fish other than salmon, as to which the Crown has special privileges.

An Act of 1770 "for the encouragement of the white herring fishery" declares that all persons employed in that fishery are to " have the free use of all ports, harbours, shores and forelands" up to highwater mark, and 100 yards beyond it, on any waste or uncultivated land, for the purpose of landing nets and stores, curing fish, and drying nets, without payment except of harbour and pier dues. This appears to give by implication a right to enter on private lands in England to the extent specified; but it is odd that there is no particular mention of owners or occupiers, nor are the fishermen expressly protected from being sued as trespassers, though they must not, under a penalty of £100, be obstructed.[2]

There were many statutes of the eighteenth and early nineteenth centuries regulating the sea-fisheries of England or of Great Britain. So far as they applied to England they were swept away, I believe without exception, by the Sea Fisheries Act of 1868.

On the Irish coast fixed or drift nets must not be used to catch herrings in the daytime, nor must any net be used (except in dredging for shell-fish) which is " covered with

---

[1] 5 & 6 Vict. c. 106, ss. 3, 4 (may be re-enactment of some older statute : the language seems modelled on that of the English local Act of James I.)

[2] 11 Geo. 3, c. 31.

canvas, hide, or other material, by which unsizeable and young fish may be taken or destroyed." Further special prohibitions may be established by means of by-laws.[1]

It must be remembered that within three miles of the coast fishermen who use nets or other instruments capable of catching salmon may come under the Salmon Fishery Acts. This has given rise to some difficulties, especially on the Welsh coast.[2]

2. *Scottish Herring Fisheries.*

The law of Scotland as to the herring fishery is contained in a number of statutes of various dates, from 1808 to 1882.[3] The earlier ones created a system of bounties, to which a system of official certificate of the herrings properly taken and cured was incidental[4]; and the system of certifying the casks of cured herrings by an official brand is still in force. All that is left of the bounties is a comparatively small annual grant for repairs of fishing-boats; and the official brand is sought merely as a kind of trade-mark, for which purpose it is found useful in the export trade. Fishermen whose business is not large enough to set up a private brand of their own which could become known in the market can by means of the Government mark, if their wares are up to the standard quality, put

---

[1] 5 & 6 Vict. c. 106, ss. 6–10, 44 & 45 Vict. c. 66 (close time for pollen).

[2] 18th Annual Report of the Inspectors of Salmon Fisheries, 1879, Appendix I. to Mr. Walpole's Report.

[3] The Acts ought to have been consolidated long ago: the older ones exist in a sort of living death, being repealed not specifically, but " in so far as necessary to give effect to," or so far as inconsistent with, the later Acts. These things are not necessarily the draftsman's or anybody's fault; but they do no credit to the law.

[4] 48 Geo. 3, c. 110, s. 35.

themselves on a level with the larger dealers; and a Select Committee which inquired into the matter in 1881 reported against the abolition of the brand. Since 1858 the expense of branding has been provided for by a fee of fourpence a barrel, so that on this point the last trace of the old bounties is removed.[1]

The Fishery Board[2] (formerly the "Commissioners of the British white herring fishery") have power to make police regulations; and there is an old rule, never expressly repealed, that the mesh of herring nets must not be less than an inch across. But this appears to be abrogated, except within three miles of the coast, by the operation of the Sea Fisheries Act of 1868; all restrictions on means of fishing beyond that limit being abolished by the Convention with France annexed to the Act, and thereby made law for British subjects. This brings us to the consideration of a fresh matter: namely, the regulation of sea fisheries by International Convention.

3. *International Conventions.*

In 1843 a Convention was made between England and France for the establishment of a common set of fishery rules on the coasts of either country; the purpose being not so much the preservation of sea-fish as the prevention of strife between fishermen of the two nations, and avoidance of difficulties about jurisdiction. In 1868 a new Convention was made, intended to supersede the former one; and being confirmed by Parliament[3] and gazetted as the Act provided, it became, and it is at present, the law governing British fishermen in British

---

[1] 21 & 22 Vict. c. 69. [2] 45 & 46 Vict. c. 78.
[3] 31 & 32 Vict. c. 45.

waters. But it was never ratified by the French Legislature, so that in French waters the old Convention of 1843 is still in force; and French fishermen cannot be proceeded against except under that Convention for offences against the fishery police of our coasts.[1]

Under the Act of 1868 all British fishing boats have to be lettered, numbered, and registered. The letters indicate a port or station having a separate collectorship of customs, and every station has its own set of numbers. The details are worked out by an Order in Council of June 18, 1869. By supplementary regulations of February 26, 1880, open boats not going out beyond the three-mile limit are exempt. Naval and revenue officers and the coastguard have by the Act and Orders in Council large powers of search and seizure, and the fines for not having the name, number, &c., duly painted on a boat may amount to £20.

The Convention lays down a number of rules (which it is impossible to abridge) as to fishing-vessels carrying lights,[2] not interfering with one another's operations, and abstaining, except in certain cases of necessity, from entering the French fishery limits.

In 1881–2 an International Conference was held at the Hague to discuss proposals for establishing a joint fishery police in the North Sea. The result was a Convention signed on May 6, 1882, by the delegates of England,

[1] See 40 & 41 Vict. c. 42, s. 15.

[2] The rule as to lights was made more specific in 1879 by an Order in Council (Regulations for preventing Collisions at Sea) under the Merchant Shipping Acts. Since September 1, 1881, till which date the operation of the Order was afterwards suspended, fishing-vessels out with drift-nets ought to carry two red lights on the mast, and trawlers a red and a green light. I doubt whether the rule is much observed in practice.

Germany, Belgium, Denmark, France and the Netherlands (power being reserved for Sweden and Norway to come in). It contains rules as to lettering, numbering, and official papers; as to the duty of boats not to interfere with each other's fishing, with a special prohibition of "any instrument or engine which serves only to cut or destroy nets;"[1] and as to the manner in which the Convention is to be carried out, and the superintendence of the fisheries exercised, by the cruisers of the several contracting Powers. This Convention has not yet acquired legal force as regards British fishermen; but it is understood that a Bill to confirm it will be introduced in the present session of Parliament. Whenever the North Sea Convention takes effect, the present anomalous relations between England and France as to the Channel fisheries will have to be reconsidered. It will be remembered that British fishermen are under one law and French under another; and an additional complication may be introduced by the limits of the new Convention, to which France is a party, overlapping those of the old ones at some points. This seems not unlikely to lead to total abrogation of the former Conventions, and the adoption, as between England and France, of the North Sea Convention (with whatever not inconsistent additions the local circumstances may require) for the Channel fisheries also.

The Treaty of Washington, made in 1871 between England and the United States, contained articles (afterwards confirmed by Parliament)[2] giving American fisher-

---

[1] Such an instrument, known as the "devil," has been used by Belgian sailors and fishermen to the great grievance of the fishermen of other nations. Its use, sale, and manufacture are now prohibited by a Belgian law of March 27, 1882.

[2] 35 & 36 Vict. c. 45. The Act seems to have been required only for the purpose of repealing earlier inconsistent statutes.

men the right of sea-fishing and landing nets and fish on
the Canadian coast, and the like right to British fishermen
on the east coast of the United States above 39° N. lat.
There are no detailed regulations or police provisions of
any kind.

4. *As to Oysters and Shell-fish.*

A close time for oyster fishing (May 1 to September 1)
has long been established in Ireland.[1] For Great Britain
as to all shell-fish, and for Ireland also as to crabs and
lobsters, the law now in force is contained in an Act of
1877 (40 & 41 Vict. c. 42). Deep-sea oysters must not be
sold or trafficked with between June 15 and August 4, nor
any other oysters between May 14 and August 4. Preserved oysters, and oysters taken in foreign waters or for
the purpose of oyster cultivation, are excepted. (Fine up
to £2 for a first offence, £10 for repeated offences, and the
oysters may be forfeited.) And the Board of Trade may,
on the application of certain local authorities, restrict or
prohibit for limited periods the taking of oysters from any
particular bed.

Crabs less than four inches and a quarter broad, and
lobsters less than eight inches long, may not be taken, sold,
or dealt with for sale. The same prohibition applies to
spawn crabs and " casters " or " soft crabs " (crabs which
have recently cast their shells.) The penalties are the same
as for selling oysters in the close season. Any crabs, however,
may be taken for bait. The Board of Trade (or in Ireland
the Inspectors of Irish Fisheries, with the approval of the
Lord Lieutenant), may restrict lobster and crab fishing
within specified areas. All shell-fish exposed for sale con-

---

[1] 5 & 6 Vict. c. 106, s. 32.

trary to the provisions of the Act may be searched for, seized, and condemned.

Under the Sea Fisheries Act of 1868, and certain Irish Acts of which the principal one was passed in 1866,[1] the Board of Trade in Great Britain, subject to confirmation by Parliament, and the Inspectors of Irish Fisheries with the approval of the Lord Lieutenant in Ireland,[2] have power to grant exclusive rights of oyster and mussel fishery, which may be revoked if the grantees do not cultivate their allotted ground properly. Power to regulate a fishery and take tolls from persons fishing in it for oysters and mussels may also be given by an order of the Board of Trade.[3] That authority issued regulations in July, 1872, setting forth the principles and conditions on which either exclusive rights of fishery or regulative powers over fisheries would be granted, and the procedure to be observed in applications and inquiries. Hardly so much use has been made of these provisions as was expected ; but it is hoped that they will in course of time produce appreciable results in increasing and cheapening the supply of oysters, though they may not avail to bring back the golden age of our fathers, when natives were a shilling a dozen. Under a recent Act [4] the Board of Trade may, for the protection of clam and bait beds, prescribe or authorise restrictions on the use of beam trawls for limited times, and within an area defined in each case by the order, anywhere in the territorial waters of Great Britain. The power can be exercised only on the

---

[1] Oyster Fishery (Ireland) Amendment Act, 1866, 29 & 30 Vict. c. 97.

[2] 32 & 33 Vict. c. 92, s. 14. The wording of the English and Irish Acts is different, but their general effect is much the same.

[3] There does not seem to be anything corresponding to this in Ireland.   [4] 44 Vict. c. 11.

application of local fishermen or authorities, and after inquiry.

As to the general policy of regulating oyster fisheries by close times and otherwise there is much difference of opinion. The evening before the opening of this Exhibition (May 11), Mr. Huxley delivered a discourse on this question at the Royal Institution, in which he called attention to the fluctuations in the supply of oysters from the principal French beds. These have long been under a system of restrictions far more severe than anything that has been or could be proposed in England; but the increase or falling off in the number of oysters taken (and in many years the variations have been very great and sudden), appears to have no intelligible relation whatever to the rules imposed by the State. In fact, there have been violent fluctuations both ways while the rules and their administration were unchanged. Mr. Huxley's conclusion is that the abundance or scarcity of oysters depends on causes which cannot be sensibly affected by any restrictive legislation. All such legislation is in itself objectionable, inasmuch as it creates new offences and tends to make the administration of justice odious, and the burden of proof is always on those who advocate it to show that its utility is so great and manifest as to outweigh the inconvenience. If Mr. Huxley's inferences from the French statistics are right (and I do not myself see the answer to them), the improvement of the oyster fisheries is to be sought, not in multiplying penal laws, which at best are troublesome to enforce and uncertain in their working, but in the judicious encouragement of oyster cultivation.

5. *Seal Fishery.*

The Greenland seal fishery does not, perhaps, come properly within the scope of this handbook. But it may be convenient to mention shortly that, in order to put a stop to the reckless destruction of the young seals, an Act was passed in 1875 (38 Vict. c. 18), which empowered the Queen in Council, being satisfied that other Powers concerned had made or would make the like regulations as to their ships and subjects, to prescribe a close time for the seal fishery between the parallels of 67° and 75° N. latitude, and the meridians of 5° E. and 17° W. longitude from Greenwich. In 1876[1] an Order in Council was made bringing the Act into operation, and fixing the 3rd of April as the earliest day in the year on which seal fishing should be lawful.

Conclusion.

We have now gone through the substance of one of those bodies of special legislation which, though their existence is hardly known except to the persons interested in their subject-matter, are of considerable extent and intricacy, and may raise important questions of general legislative policy. Thus it is evident that in the case of the fishery laws the question of interference with private discretion by the authority of the State has constantly to be decided one way or the other. In dealing with fresh-water fisheries the tendency of modern law-making has been to impose new restrictions, in dealing with sea-fisheries to remove old ones. There is not necessarily any inconsistency in this, for the circumstances and the

[1] Nov. 28 : see the order in Maude and Pollock's Merchant Shipping, 4th ed., Appendix, p. 104.

purposes of the law are widely different. Particular questions of no small delicacy may, however, occur in the administration of the law. The State has decided that salmon rivers are worth preserving at the cost of some compulsion and restriction ; and few persons who are not extreme partisans of the individual citizen's freedom to do as he pleases will object to this in principle. But how far are we to go in each case ? Is the preservation always worth the cost ? Paper-mills and salmon, for example, cannot thrive on the same water ; nor can it be said in every case that the paper-mill may go where there are no. salmon, for not all river water is fit to make paper with. Are we then bound to sacrifice a great paper-mill for a small and poor salmon river, as might conceivably be the result in some cases of a strict execution of the Salmon Fishery Acts? These are the problems which English statesmen and legislators have hitherto refused, and most wisely refused, to deal with by general formulas, and have left to be worked out by the good sense and discretion of the persons concerned. A lawmaker who thinks and speaks as if he were dealing with a nation of fools will never make good laws ; a passion for formulas is the mark not of an exact but of a petty mind, and is capable of becoming the ruin of legislation and politics. It is enough for us, as regards the matter in hand, to know that our fishery laws, since their improvement was seriously taken up some twenty years ago, have on the whole worked well and prevented much mischief. From a lawyer's point of view (and, I should think, from the point of view of any one who desires to understand them) there is much to be mended in their form. But with all their faults they are a fairly creditable specimen of the manner in which that complex and overburdened instrument of government, the Parliament of the United Kingdom, contrives as it were from hand to mouth, and almost without knowing it, to keep abreast of the multifarious wants and grievances of a state of society which its founders could never have imagined.

LONDON: PRINTED BY WILLIAM CLOWES AND SONS, LIMITED, STAMFORD STREET AND CHARING CROSS.

CPSIA information can be obtained at www.ICGtesting.com
Printed in the USA
BVOW09s0959230915

419332BV00016B/222/P